Copyright 2015 © Peggy Edw

All Rights Reserved

ISBN-13: 978-1516923229

ISBN-10: 1516923227

peggypedwards@gmail.com

Peggy P Edwards

I was born in Mexico City, Mexico and raised a polyglot; living and learning among several cultures and languages.

I ran the gamut teaching University, Adult Education (ESL and SSL), High School, Elementary and Preschool, focusing on culture and language.

I received a Bachelor of Arts from Southern Methodist University in Dallas and a Master of Arts from the University of Wisconsin, Madison. I was certified to teach in Texas and California.

CEO of American Immigrant Foundation, I am now retired and President of the Village Publishing Club.

I like to draw, play music on my ukulele, and I'm an apprentice videographer.

"Alfabeto Crossover Alphabet" crosses you over easily from English to Spanish or from Spanish to English. A CD is available for pronunciation, but even better; invite a Spanish speaker to crossover to Spanish using "Alfabeto Crossover Alphabet."   The back cover is a coloring page – can you find all the letters?

ACA books also cross you over to French: English/Spanish, English/French, Spanish/French. The creation and illustrations are mine. I also published "Lalalandia" - eight mystical, magical, bilingual stories.

ACA Spanish Pronunciation Guide

A	ah		O	oh
B	b		P	p
C	s, k			
Ch	ch		Q	k (always followed by a silent u)
D	d		R	rrr, rr
E	eh		S	s
F	f		T	t
G	h (hot), g (goat)		U	w
H	(silent)		V	v
I	e (as in meet)		W	
J	h (as in hot)		X	h (as in hot)
K	k		Y	y (as in yes)
L	l		Z	s
Ll	y (as in yes)			
M	m			
N	n			
Ñ	gn			

Vowels have only one sound. Get help to pronounce the R and D-sounds which do not exist in English

ANGEL   ÁNGEL

BABY **BEBÉ**

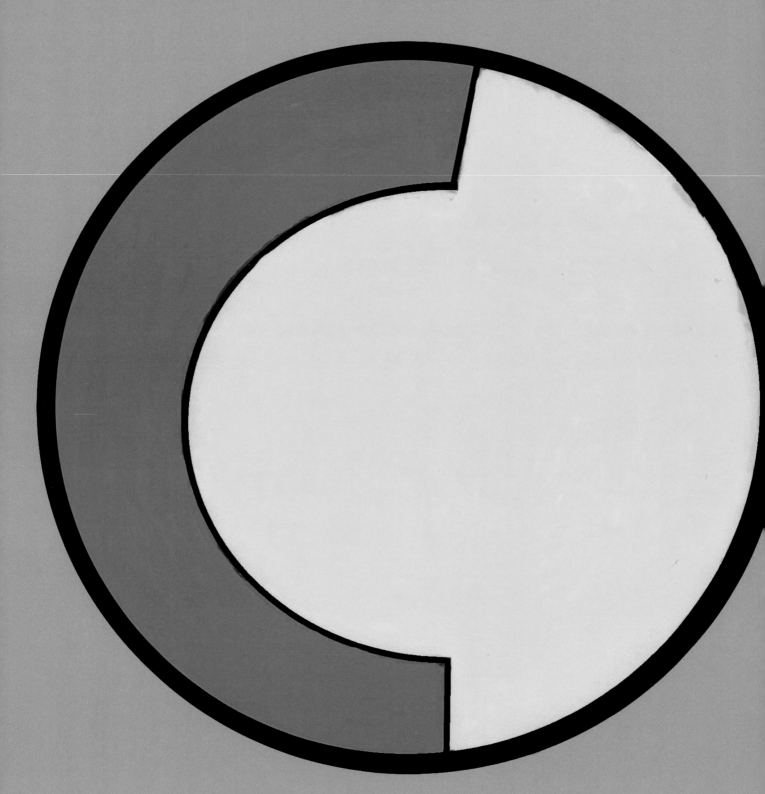

DINOSAUR DINOSAURIO

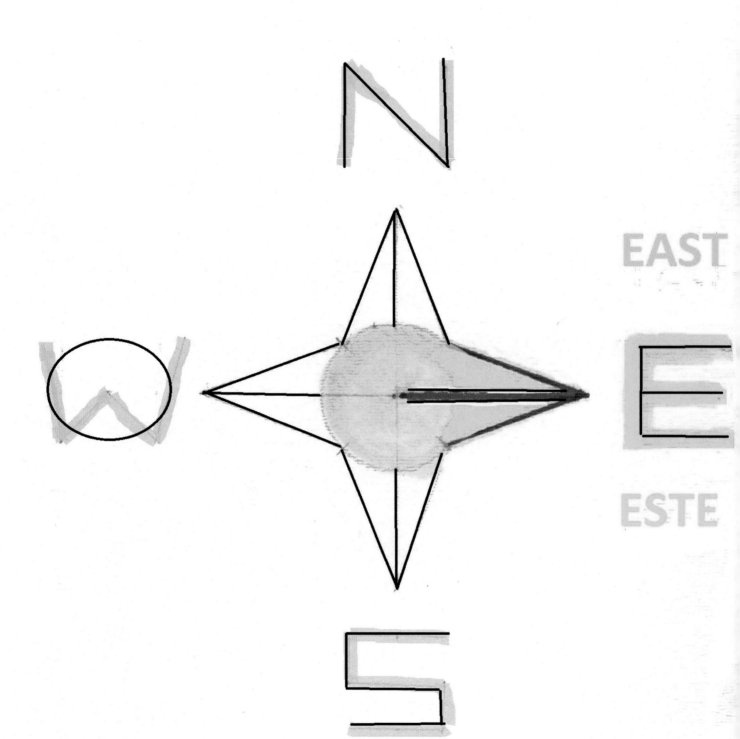

HIPPOPOTAMUS
HIPOPÓTAMO

ISLAND ISLA

JAGUAR

KIMONO

LION LEÓN

MOUNTAIN   MONTAÑA

NORTH NORTE

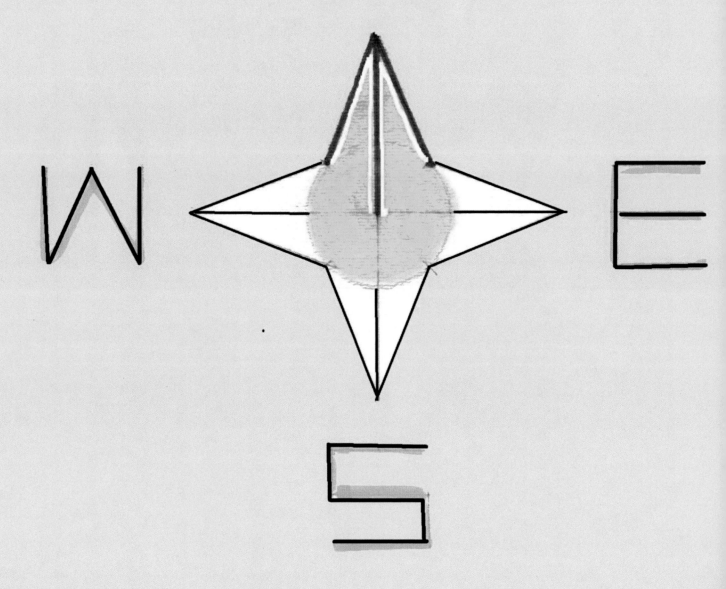

ÑANDÚ

PYRAMID

PIRÁMIDE

QUETZAL

RIVER RÍO

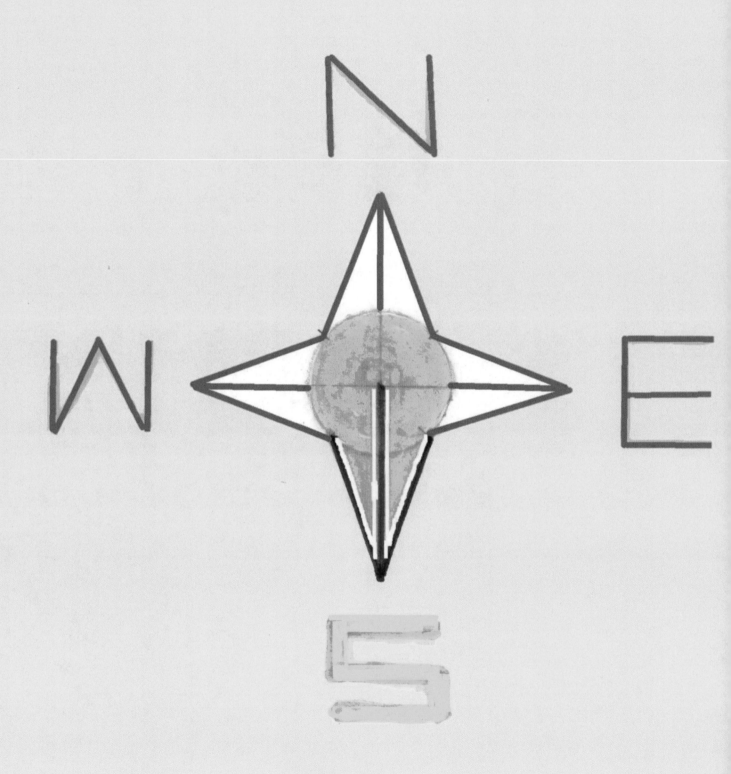

SOUTH SUR

TRAIN
TREN

TUNNEL
TÚNEL

UNICORN UNICORNIO

VIOLIN   VIOLÍN

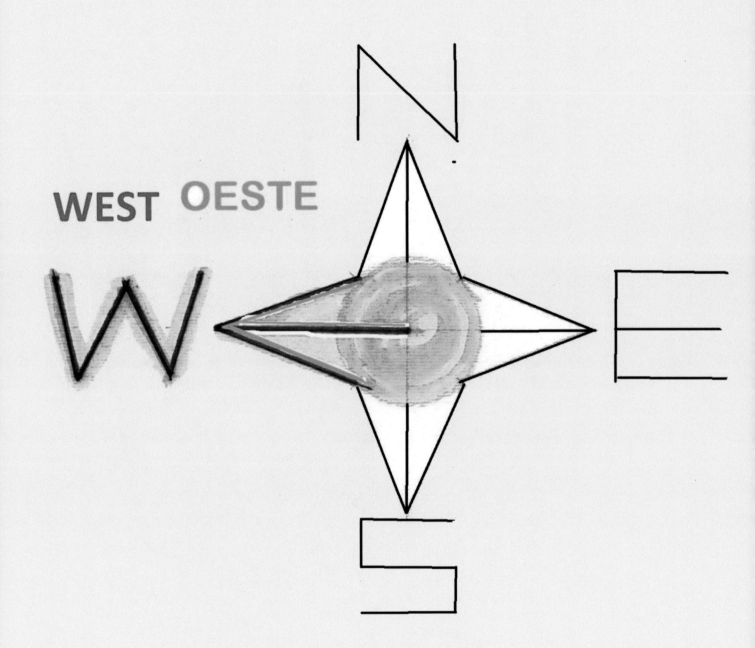

WEST OESTE

XYLOPHONE
XILÓFONO

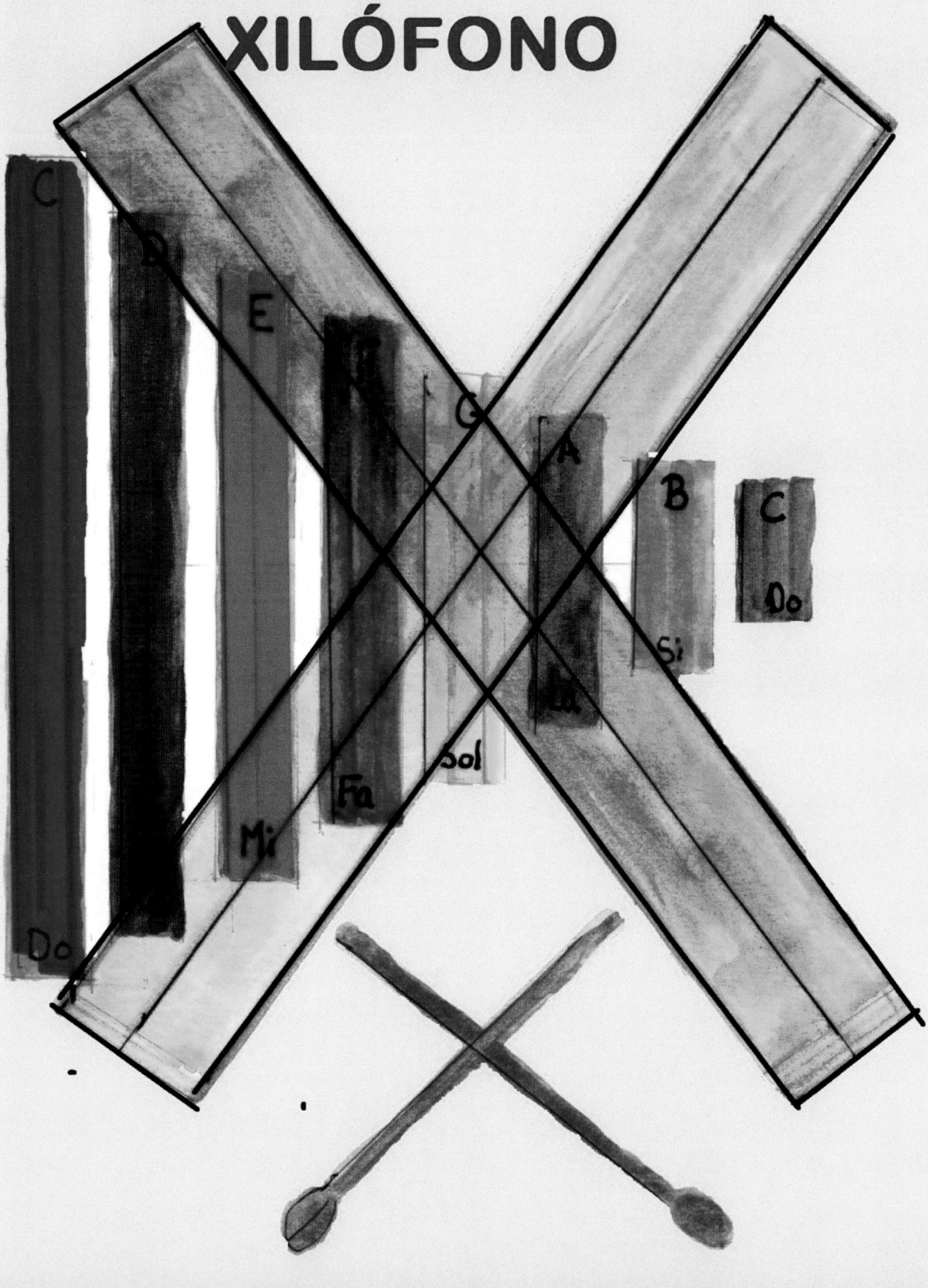

YOYO

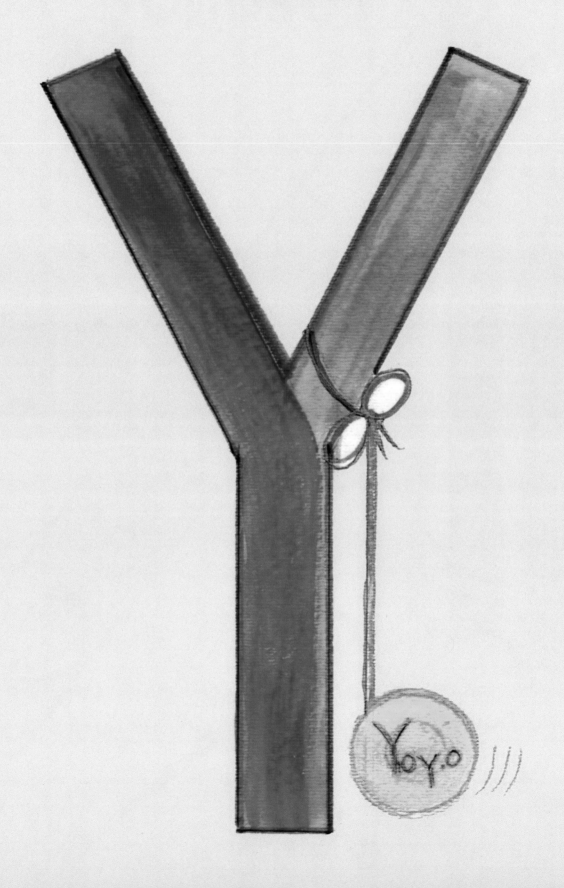

ZOO **ZOOLÓGICO**

Made in the USA
Las Vegas, NV
27 February 2022

44698385R00021